MOUNT ST. HELENS REGION

RIVER

Creek

STRAWBERRY MTN.

GOAT MTN.

BLACK MTN.

MT. VENUS

MT. MARGARET BACKCOUNTRY

Creek

MT. MARGARET

BEAR MEADOW

504

Creek

ELK ROCK

ST. HELENS LAKE

LANGE MINE

SWEDEN MINE

TOUTLE

RIVER

Coldwater

BOY SCOUT CAMP

YMCA CAMP

HARMONY FALLS

Clearwater

504

SPIRIT LAKE

DUCK BAY

GE

Herrington Creek

SPOTTED BUCK MTN.

SPUD MTN.

LANGE HOMESTEAD

EPISCOPAL CHURCH CAMP

Bean

Creek

Smith

FLOATING ISLAND LAVA FLOW

TIMBERLINE VIEWPOINT

GOAT ROCKS

SUGAR BOWL

FORSYTH GLACIER

SMITH CREEK BUTTE

Creek

TALUS GLACIER

THE BOOT

DOGS HEAD

PUMICE BUTTE

APE CANYON

MOUNT ST. HELENS

ELK MTN.

Creek

GOAT MTN.

Fossil

Creek

MUDDY

RIVER

ELK MTN.

APE CAVE

MARBLE MTN.

MERRILL LAKE

Ole's Cave

AREA MAY 18, 1980

RIVER

YALE LAKE

SWIFT RESERVOIR

2   3   4   5 Miles

SCALE

MOUNT
ST. HELENS

For the past century Mount St. Helens was primarily famed for its beauty. Although not as high as the other major volcanic cones that crown the Cascade Range, St. Helens' youthful symmetry stood out among the older, more weathered peaks. Especially in winter, with a glistening white coat of snow, the mountain hovered over the dark, evergreen horizon like a mirage, too perfect to exist except in our minds.

Mount St. Helens from Bear Cove, Spirit Lake. *Photo by David Muench.*

A new eruptive cycle began in March 1980, and two months later a tremendous explosion blew the top off Mount St. Helens, reshaped Spirit Lake, and spread ash across the land. A jagged, rapidly-changing crater replaced the oval glacier-topped crown; and the surrounding landscape was suddenly and dramatically changed.

The massive eruption on May 18, 1980. *Photo by Glen Finch.*

The cycle continues on. When Mount St. Helens will erupt again is not predictable, at least not yet; but erupt again it will. In the years and centuries to come, the present landscape—now usually described as "devastated"—will evolve into friendly, lush forests and meadows—and then back to dust and ash, and on and on.

The truncated cone of Mount St. Helens. *Photo by Al Hayward.*

MOUNT
ST. HELENS

A CHANGING LANDSCAPE

TEXT BY CHUCK WILLIAMS
INTRODUCTION BY RAY ATKESON

GRAPHIC ARTS CENTER PUBLISHING COMPANY
PORTLAND, OREGON

INTERNATIONAL STANDARD BOOK NUMBER 0-912856-63-7
LIBRARY OF CONGRESS CATALOG CARD NUMBER 80-83472
COPYRIGHT ©1980 BY GRAPHIC ARTS CENTER PUBLISHING CO.
P.O. BOX 10306 • PORTLAND, OREGON 97210 • 503/224-7777

STAFF FOR THIS BOOK:
EDITOR-IN-CHARGE • DOUGLAS A. PFEIFFER
TEXT • CHUCK WILLIAMS
EDITING • SPENCER GILL
DESIGN • ROBERT REYNOLDS
CARTOGRAPHY • JUDITH A. FARMER
TYPESETTER • PAUL O. GIESEY/ADCRAFTERS
PRINTER • GRAPHIC ARTS CENTER
BINDERY • LINCOLN AND ALLEN
PRINTED IN THE UNITED STATES OF AMERICA
SECOND PRINTING

Special Consultants:

Dr. Gilbert T. Benson
Associate Professor of Geology
Earth Sciences Department
Portland State University
Portland, Oregon

Dr. Donald B. Lawrence
Professor Emeritus
Department of Botany
University of Minnesota
St. Paul, Minnesota

Pages 8-9: Afternoon sunlight on the west wall of Mount St. Helens. *Photo by Gary Braasch.* **Opposite:** In the Gifford Pinchot National Forest of southwest Washington, beargrass blooms on a ridge below 9,677-foot Mount St. Helens, one of sixteen major volcanic peaks in the Cascade Range. Indian women gathered beargrass stalks as one of the many fibers used in making and decorating baskets. *Photo by David Muench.* **Overleaf:** Early fall reveals the features of the north face of the mountain. Prominent points are (left to right): Dog's Head, Forsyth Glacier, Sugar Bowl (bottom-center), Little Lizard, Big Lizard, The Boot (the talus formation near the summit) and Goat Rocks (partly hidden by a tree). *Photo by Ray Atkeson.*

INTRODUCTION

My infatuation with Mount St. Helens began in 1928 when I spent a weekend at the Portland YMCA Camp on the south shore of Spirit Lake. Navigating the old road through timber from Castle Rock to Spirit Lake was an adventure in itself at that time: the narrow, muddy road twisted and squirmed through miles and miles of virgin forest and sometimes seemed impenetrable and, in fact, exacted a toll as tree trunks, roots, and rocks disputed the right of way. I recall the main topic of conversation around the evening campfire was tales of those who became stuck in one or more of the numerous mud holes or miscalculated the width of the road on some particularly narrow turn.

Upon arrival at the Portland YMCA Camp, I was surprised and, to say the least, disappointed to find that after all that trip I still was unable to see Mount St. Helens. The first summer camp was conducted in 1909 and a special use permit was issued in 1911 for a permanent campsite on the south end of the lake. Even in 1928, it seemed an unlikely place to lure young people for a long sojourn on the damp, mossy forest floor with giant trees so dense and tall that sunlight could not penetrate to the camp. The view of the Mount Margaret Range, flecked with patches of snow, alpine meadows and rugged peaks to the north, was inspiring, but it wasn't Mount St. Helens. Boats were available to reach sunnier spots across the lake and to view the volcanic cone of St. Helens. Camp activities with daytime hikes along beautiful forest trails soon cleared the mind of any adverse impressions.

In 1946 YMCA executives established the new Camp Meehan in a sunnier, but more secluded location in the less-dense forests straddling Paradise Creek on the northern shore of the eastern arm of the lake. The location was ideal, with a pumice sand and gravel beach where shallow waters were warmed by full sunlight. Access was mainly by boat across the lake. The lack of roads and a scarcity of passersby on nearby trails added to the desired seclusion. Later, other youth camps for the Boy Scouts, Girl Scouts and the Southwest Washington YMCA were developed.

During ensuing years, Spirit Lake became a favorite destination whenever I had time to make the trip. My first climb of Mount St. Helens was, I believe, in the spring of 1931 via the Dog's Head route. The road ended at the lake in those days, though there was an old wagon road to Timberline, a distance of three miles. It was a beautiful spring climb and was uneventful except for the return to Timberline. We had a glorious glissade down the smooth, unbroken snow slope, sometimes on our feet with weight on our alpenstocks, but more often on the seat of our pants. All went well for my late wife, Mira, and me; but our companions sped past Dog's Head without realizing it, staying on open snow to the south and ending up near the Plains of Abraham, a couple extra miles of walking across uneven terrain and soft snow back to our point of ascent.

In the summer of 1932, Mira and I joined five others for another ascent of St. Helens. We started long before dawn under heavy overcast clouds which produced enough drizzle to discourage most sensible outdoor enthusiasts. Just about sunrise we suddenly found ourselves above a turbulent sea of clouds as we reached the Dog's Head. Beautiful stratus clouds above reflected sunrise colors and silhouetted Mt. Adams to the east and Mt. Rainier many miles to the north. The summit goal was forgotten for an hour or so of exciting photography (black and white only, unfortunately). The clouds above and below slowly melted away, and brilliant sunshine favored our arrival at the summit.

As the road improved over the years, our visits to Spirit Lake became more frequent. Logging operations encircled the mountain and timber access roads penetrated more remote areas about the peak. Long before that, we had made frequent visits to the south side of St. Helens to explore the lava caves and climb Mount Mitchell, a 4,000 ft. peak accessible from the Lewis River in the vicinity of the present site of Swift Reservoir. A hand-propelled basket-ferry suspended from a long cable was used to cross the river to the trail head. Almost constant vistas of Mount St. Helens were enjoyed through the trees on the climb to the crest of Mount Mitchell, where a panorama of mountains, forests, and river valleys, as well as distant peaks of the Cascades extended before us.

Mira, our young daughter Eleanor and I enjoyed a couple of vacations in a rustic cabin at Harmony Falls on the east arm of the lake. It was a marvelous, somewhat secluded resort consisting of a small lodge, a few cabins clustered around a timberbound waterfall and babbling stream, all with magnificent tree-framed views of the lake and mountain. Owners Jack and Tressa Nelson and his sister, Ruby, were famous for their hospitality and gourmet meals — so famous that countless visitors drove to Spirit Lake just to enjoy a Saturday or Sunday afternoon dinner with the Nelsons. Harmony Falls was accessible from roads-end on the south shore of the lake by hiking a three-mile scenic forest trail or by simply cranking the ancient telephone at a boat landing and waiting for Jack to come across the lake to pick up his guests. I'll long remember the exciting illusionary phenomenon which impressed me on my first ride in Jack Nelson's launch to Harmony Falls — an illusion that I am sure thousands of boaters on Spirit Lake have enjoyed. As the boat gathered speed and reached a distance of perhaps two hundred yards from the south boat landing, the brilliant glacier-clad crest of Mount St. Helens began to appear above the dense evergreen trees. The top of the mountain seemed to grow skyward as we moved farther out on the lake and soon the great glacier-clad cone became a whole glorious mountain — a spectacle that never ceased to thrill me. It was an exciting introduction to another visit to Spirit Lake.

In addition to the picture possibilities provided as one climbed Mount St. Helens, the timbered shoreline of Spirit Lake offered opportunity for many scenes of varied nature. The trail along the east shore of the lake sometimes dipped down close to the water, other times traveled over knolls affording panoramic views of the lake. It wasn't until one reached the area of Harmony Falls that pictures of the mountain itself were available. Here, giant evergreens and some

Henry Warre painted this 1844 view of Mount St. Helens from the Cowlitz farms of the Hudson's Bay Company. Warre and his companion, Vavasour, traveled throughout the Northwest posing as artists and scientists, but they were actually spying for the British government. Warre did, however, leave to posterity some noteworthy paintings, including one of Mount St. Helens erupting and another which shows that Goat Rocks had already formed on the mountain by 1844. *Courtesy American Antiquarian Society.*

huge cottonwoods at the mouth of Harmony Creek framed exciting vistas of the mountain and the lake.

View points of the mountain from other areas on the shoreline were best reached by boat. One spot I particularly favored was a rocky point where a picturesque cottage belonging to John C. Meehan commanded a superlative view. Lured there time and again at various seasons, I was able to capture a large number of pleasing photographs.

The timber along the lake was so dense and hugged the shoreline of the water so tightly that it was usually difficult to find room to compose a picture including both lakeshore and mountain. One favored place in the early days was where Bear Creek flowed into the west arm of the lake. Here, in the thirties, a motion picture company on location felled a giant fir tree toward the lake. The resulting movie footage was spectacular: the tree slowly tumbling toward the lake to reveal the mountain, which, until then, had not been visible because of the dense forest growth. The mountain was, from that time on, framed by large evergreens on each side. Later, on many occasions, I took advantage of this tree-framed setting to photograph Mount St. Helens and Spirit Lake.

In later years, as youth camps began to develop around the north shore, new picture opportunities were available as timber was cleared to make space for camp activities. The usual tranquillity of early morning was especially rewarding when the crisp, clear atmosphere and the mirror-like lake surface best reflected the sunrise-tinted image of St. Helens. Only the dip of our paddle in the water, the awakening sounds from youth camps around the 12-mile lakeshore or a melodious call of birds disturbed the quiet solitude. Frequently the lake reflections would hold until mid-day, especially in autumn months, when huckleberry, blueberry and vine maple foliage added their autumn tints to the pristine beauty. During the longer days of June, the sunset glow enhanced the mountain's beauty as it illuminated Wishbone Glacier on the northwest slope of the peak.

The Mt. Margaret country, reached by trails along the east and west sides of the lake, lured many hikers and packers. It was a high, rugged area of open alpine meadows, with a sprinkling of picturesque timberline-like trees and jagged, rugged peaks. Nestled in a bowl on the west end of the Mt. Margaret Range was St. Helens Lake, often remaining frozen or with floating ice on the water until early summer. All of this wild, open region around Mt. Margaret and other peaks unfurled magnificent views of Mount St. Helens. Unfortunately, Spirit Lake was so close to the base of the range that only portions of it were visible from any one point. Fine views of Mt. Adams and Mt. Rainier were also available from Mt. Margaret. The setting often included small lakes on the north slopes of the range as foreground interest for pictures of Mount Rainier and the Goat Rocks Wilderness Area. These high meadows were among the few such alpine areas in the vicinity of Mount St. Helens where wild flowers grew to any extent. It was a great place for two or three day photography trips from the base camp at Spirit Lake.

We also used canoes and boats with outboard motors to reach favorite places around the lake and take advantage of changing lights and colors during the days and seasons. Harry Truman, a Spirit Lake resident for over 50 years, was proprietor of Mount St. Helens Lodge on the south shore and often supplied us with our water transportation. On one occasion Harry miscalculated his jump into a canoe we had pushed toward the dock. He landed in the bow and was promptly flipped into the lake. At first we thought his splashing in the water was just a show, but when he sank below the surface, I dived down and finally, with Mira's help, managed to get him up on the dock. With a little pumping we helped him get rid of some extra water and start the air into his lungs again. He told us then, that for all his years of living at the lake, he had never learned to swim because the water was "too damned cold."

The trail to Timberline became a road, then a highway; and logging access roads reached eastward into once-virgin forests. Timberline, three miles above the lake, was developing into a popular winter playground with advent of year-round access. The mountain became surrounded with logging operations, and outdoor activities increased in the Spirit Lake area. With power dam construction on the Lewis River south of the mountain, paved highways and gravel spur roads opened up new recreational opportunities for boaters, campers, hunters and fishermen.

As the years passed, thousands of people became acquainted with Spirit Lake and one of the most beautiful mountains in the world: a mountain that I frequently referred to as being "friendly." But the experiences of the early days will not be forgotten by any who were fortunate to know Spirit Lake and Mount St. Helens and the splendid solitude that was so much a part of visits to the area while it was less accessible.

Many have known the mountain longer and more intimately than I, especially those who have been closely associated with the lodges and youth camps on the shores of Spirit Lake. All who visited Mount St. Helens and Spirit Lake have great memories. Yet it is the sketches of explorers, canvases of painters, and images by photographers that best share the memories of this lovely area with those who were not fortunate enough to have visited it prior to the May 18, 1980 eruption.

Here is a book filled with beauty, for Mount St. Helens was truly a magnificent mountain in a pristine setting. But it is also a fascinating visual and written record of a changing landscape. Through these pages you are offered a rare glimpse of nature — one that reveals Mount St. Helens as a volcano in a continuing state of transition.

— Ray Atkeson

Paul Kane, a Canadian artist, visited the Northwest in 1847. While at the mouth of the Lewis River, he wrote: "There was not a cloud visible in the sky at the time I commenced my sketch, and not a breath of air was perceptible; suddenly a stream of white smoke shot up from the crater of the mountain and hovered a short time over its summit; it then settled down like a cap." The top painting records this venting of steam. Kane painted the night-time scene after he had returned to Canada, basing it on second-hand reports of the 1842-1844 eruptions. *Above, top: Courtesy Stark Museum of Art. Above: Courtesy Royal Ontario Museum.*

A member of the Embody party (1897 or 1898) peers into Ape Canyon on the southeast side of the mountain. The narrow canyon received its present name in 1924, when six miners claimed to have slain a "large hairy ape" whose body allegedly rolled into the ravine. Thus began the legend of Bigfoot. *Photo by Charles W. Embody / Courtesy Donald B. Lawrence Collection.*

KEEPER OF THE FIRE

Human occupation near Mount St. Helens is a recent phenomenon. The volcano is young and active, and the Native Americans of the region avoided Spirit Lake and Mount St. Helens, especially above timberline. When Canadian painter Paul Kane traveled through the Northwest in the mid-1800s, he sketched eruptions from the Columbia and Cowlitz Rivers, but was unable to find an Indian willing to guide him to Spirit Lake and the volcano.

Mount St. Helens rose in a rugged, little-used land between three diverse prehistoric cultures: the Salish-speaking people of Puget Sound and what became northern Washington, the Sahaptin-language people of the plateau east of the Cascades, and the Chinookan-speaking residents of the lower Columbia. Important Chinook settlements near the volcano included the Cathlapotle village at the mouth of the Lewis River and the Skilloot villages near the mouth of the Cowlitz. The Indian peoples known as the Cowlitz were united politically but were actually two distinct groups. The residents along the lower and middle Cowlitz River were Coast Salish, while the Taidnapam, or Upper Cowlitz, who lived directly north (and probably south) of the volcano, increasingly spoke Sahaptin, although Salish culture and bloodlines continued to dominate. The Klickitat Indians, who resided between Mount St. Helens, Mount Adams and the Columbia Gorge, spoke Sahaptin and were closely related to the Yakimas.

Since the area around Mount St. Helens was a "melting pot," most of its prehistoric residents were at least bilingual; many were trilingual. The Chinooks lived primarily on salmon, but the Cowlitz, who had fewer good fisheries in their territory, were more dependent upon hunting, especially for deer. The Chinooks and Cowlitz also collected berries and roots around Mount St. Helens. These plant foods constituted an even larger part of the diet of the Klickitats and other plateau tribes to the east.

Each tribe in the vicinity of Mount St. Helens had its own name for the peak and its own legends regarding the mountain's history. *Loo-wit,* now the most commonly used "Indian" name for Mount St. Helens, is probably anglicized; other names include *Lawelatla* ("One From Whom Smoke Comes") and *Tah-one-lat-clah* ("Fire Mountain").

The best-known legend involving the volcano is the story of the Bridge of the Gods and the creation of the Columbia Gorge. In most versions, Mount Hood and Mount Adams, sons of the Great Spirit, fought over a beautiful female mountain. The brothers shook the earth, blocked the sunlight, threw fire at each other, burned the forests, drove off the animals and covered the plants needed by the people with ash. The fight cracked the Cascade Range, forming a canyon and a tunnel which emptied the huge lake east of the mountains. The Great Spirit returned and was furious. He left the Bridge of the Gods, the stone arch over the Columbia River, as a monument to peace and placed an elderly, weathered female mountain, Loo-wit, at the bridge as a peacemaker — and as a reminder to the brothers of how transient youthful beauty is. Loo-wit

was the keeper of the fire, which had been stolen from atop Wy-east (Mount Hood) by Coyote the Trickster.

Slowly the scars of the battle healed; the green forests returned, and the brothers again wore white coats. But after many years of happiness, jealousy between the brothers again erupted into battle. The earth shook so hard that the Bridge of the Gods fell into the river, creating the Cascades of the Columbia. Loo-wit tried to stop the fight, but she was badly battered and fell into the river. As a reward for her bravery, the Great Spirit gave Loo-wit one wish; she replied that she would like to be young and beautiful again. The Great Spirit granted her wish but told her that her mind would have to remain old; Loo-wit replied that she preferred it that way. Since nearly all of her friends had passed away and had been replaced by young upstarts, she moved off by herself, away from the other mountains.

In some versions of this much-altered legend, Mount St. Helens is the beautiful woman that the brothers fought over; in others, she is the hot-tempered wife of Mount Hood. Among the Cowlitz who lived northwest of the volcano, the battle was between Mount St. Helens and Mount Rainier.

The natives who lived along the streams below Mount St. Helens seasonally visited the mountain's wooded flanks to hunt, fish and collect plants; temporary camps were made during these expeditions. However, only youths on spirit quests — those who were seeking exceptionally powerful guardian spirits—ventured as far up as timberline. Spirit Lake was off-limits; it was the home of an outlaw band of demons, a Hell of sorts. The salmon in the lake were thought by many to be the ghosts of the evilest people that ever lived. If one of these wicked *Seatco* were caught, the others would murder a dozen people from the fisherman's tribe. The local Indians claimed that near Spirit Lake loud moans often filled the air and waterfalls could be heard in areas where none existed. Later versions of these legends often claimed that the evil spirits at the lake were punishing the local tribes for allowing the white people into the land.

European exploration of the Northwest began in earnest near the end of the 18th century, when the abundance of fur-bearing animals, especially sea otters and beavers, attracted trading ships from around the world. A British explorer, George Vancouver, sighted Mount St. Helens in 1792 and gave the peak its present name in honor of a noted British diplomat, Alleyne Fitzherbert, the Baron of St. Helens (a city near Liverpool).

The next *recorded* sighting of Mount St. Helens was by the Lewis and Clark Expedition in 1805. Lt. William Clark was fascinated by the mountain; he wrote that it rose "something in the form of a Sugar lofe" and was the "most noble looking object of its kind in nature." During the years between the visits of Vancouver and Clark, Mount St. Helens had a major eruption; but it went unmentioned by the fur traders, possibly because of the region's notoriously cloudy weather. However, the huge eruption around 1802 spread ash across what later became eastern Washington and Idaho, and the ashfall be-

E.b.S.

The entrance of COLUMBIA RIVER CAPE DISAPOINTMENT in Lat.^de 46.° 19 ′N^th and Long.^de 236.°6′ East bearing N^th 75 E.! 4 Miles distant Var^tn 18.° Eas^ly.

The second known drawing of Mount St. Helens (directly above "E. b S.") shows a shortened summit, probably due to a cloud cover at the time it was sketched by Harry Humphrys, a member of George Vancouver's survey of the Northwest Coast in 1792. *Courtesy G. T. Benson Collection.*

came part of the oral tradition of the affected tribes. In the mid-1800s, missionaries at the Tshimakain Mission (near Spokane) recorded stories told among the local tribes about the time, decades earlier, when ash "fell to the depth of six inches" during "a very long night with heavy thunder." Scientific evidence only recently confirmed that earlier turn-of-the-century eruption.

The Kalispel of northern Idaho told of the afternoon when "it rained cinders and fire." The tribe "supposed that the sun had burnt up, and that there was an end of all things. The next morning, when the sun arose, they were so delighted as to have a great dance and a feast."

The Sanpoil were so frightened by the ashfall that "the whole summer was spent in praying. The people even danced — something they never did except in winter." The nearby Nespelem were afraid that the ash "prognosticated evil"; they "prayed to the 'dry snow,' called it 'Chief' and 'Mystery' and asked it to explain itself and tell why it came."

A Spokane chief told members of the United States' 1841 Wilkes Expedition that his people thought the ash meant "the world was falling to pieces." The most respected medicine man assured the tribe that the world was not ending—at least not yet. But he warned them that: "Soon there will come from the rising sun a different kind of men from any you have yet seen, who will bring with them a book, and will teach you everything, and after that the world will fall to pieces." Other Spokane accounts told of a strong earthquake and the starvation of many people during the harsh winter that followed the ashfall.

The world soon fell apart for the Native Americans near Mount St. Helens; they were decimated by the diseases brought by the white newcomers. The combination of a smallpox epidemic about 1790 and a wave of malaria or flu around 1830 killed over ninety percent of the natives living west of the mountain; measles increased the toll. The more-nomadic tribes east of the Cascades were generally less affected, and the Klickitats increasingly used the lower Lewis River watershed and replaced the Chinooks as the region's most important traders, the "middle-men" between coastal tribes and the famous Long Narrows/Celilo Falls trade mart.

The Canadian North West Company forced out U.S. and European competitors and controlled the fur trade until 1821, when it was absorbed — under orders from Britain — by the Hudson's Bay Company, which moved the regional headquarters upriver to Fort Vancouver. In the 1830s Nathaniel Wyeth and other entrepreneurs from the U.S. failed in their efforts to compete with the British in the Northwest — but brought with them Protestant missionaries who, as it turned out, were better colonizers than preachers. The Catholics countered by sending missionaries to British outposts, including the Hudson's Bay Company farms at Cowlitz Landing (near Toledo), the start of the overland portage trail which connected the Columbia River system to the Nisqually arm of Puget Sound.

The pioneers from the United States, who made the great trek across the Oregon Trail and settled in the valleys west of the Cascade Range, ultimately brought an end to British domination of the Northwest. Hall J. Kelley, the most vocal promoter of U.S. colonization of the Northwest, wanted to change the name of the Cascades to the Presidential Range; under his scheme, St. Helens would have become Mount Washington.

The first recorded eruption of Mount St. Helens was in 1835, when Meredith Gairdner, a physician at Fort Vancouver, noted ashfall during a couple of unusually hazy days. He found "the mountain destitute of its cover of everlasting snow" and saw what "appeared to be lava flows" through his telescope. Gairdner wrote that there was a similar period of haze in 1831, which, in retrospect, he thought was also an eruption.

Then on November 22, 1842, Reverend Josiah L. Parrish was in a meeting at Champoeg, the site of the Methodist mission on the lower Willamette River. He stepped outside and noticed that Mount St. Helens was erupting, but when he told Jason Lee and the other missionaries still inside, they "laughed the idea to scorn." Finally, the men stepped outside, where they "saw arising from its summit, immense and beautiful scrolls of what seemed to be pure white steam, which rose many degrees into the heavens," while down next to "the mountain's top the substance was black as ink." The following day, Parrish "noticed that she had changed her snowy dress of pure white for somber black mantle." He later wrote that "flames were seen for a long time issuing from a crater on the south side of the mountain, two-thirds of the way up." Further eruptions over the next few days dumped ash from the Pacific Ocean to The Dalles, where "the winds had wafted its ashes to the door of the missionaries." Daniel Lee, the founder of the Wascopam Mission at The Dalles, noted the smell of sulphur and wrote that "a dark, heavy cloud was seen rising in the direction of Mount St. Helens," but "no special remark was excited by this fact." However, the missionaries arose the next morning to find that "the ejected ashes were falling with a mist-like appearance, covering the leaves, fences, and stones with a light, fine, gritty substance, in appearance like hoar frost, some specimens of which were collected." These specimens were given to U.S. Army explorer John C. Fremont the following year, but he later lost them during a flash flood in Kansas on the way back to the East.

Another Methodist missionary, Elijah White, wrote that "immense quantities of melted lava were rolling down its sides, and inundating the plains below." This account is no doubt exaggerated, but there are other eyewitness reports of lava flows during this series of eruptions. An early pioneer reported that an Indian deer hunter had badly burned a leg trying to jump a lava flow and was treated at Fort Vancouver, but the doctors at the fort were later unable to recall such an event. There were numerous reports of dead fish in the Toutle River during these eruptions, and a French-Canadian voyageur living along the lower Toutle claimed that "the light from the burning volcano was so intense that one could see to

The Sweden Mine on Paradise Creek was already a relic in 1938, when this photograph was taken. The original claim was filed by Andy Olsen in 1891 and was later worked by Dr. Henry Coe for a brief time, but produced only a few cars of low-grade copper ore. *Courtesy U. S. Forest Service.*

pick up a pin in the grass at midnight near his cabin, which is some 20 miles distant." The Oregon City *Spectator* reported that both Mount St. Helens and Mount Baker (in northern Washington) erupted in 1850.

The major eruptions of this cycle occurred during the years of 1842-44, but sporadic volcanic activity lasted until 1857, when Mount St. Helens finally calmed down again. Even before the 123-year period of relative dormancy began, the first party of climbers reached the summit. In the summer of 1853, Captain George McClellan and his U.S. Army survey expedition (including geologist George Gibbs) cleared out the old Klickitat Trail, which went up the Lewis River drainage and crossed the Cascades south of Mount Adams; he found some native villages along the Lewis and a fishing camp above the present town of Yacolt. At this time, there were still Cowlitz Indians living up the Lewis River who had never seen white people. Most newcomers went to the Willamette Valley, although a few settled along the Cowlitz River and the overland portage. (There were settlers at Woodland as early as 1845.) Another trans-Cascade route, the Yakima Trail, went up the Cowlitz River and crossed the divide north of Mount Adams.

The earliest recorded ascent of Mount St. Helens was in August 1853 by a group of four men led by Thomas J. Dryer, the first editor of *The Oregonian.* The two-week trip from Vancouver was made by horseback along the newly-cleared Lewis River trail, then by foot up the south slope, which Dryer called "sublimely grand and impossible to describe." Nevertheless, the newspaperman wrote of "blackened piles of lava which were thrown into ridges hundreds of feet high in every imaginable shape of primitive formation." Dryer felt that the mountain was "seeming to lift its head above and struggling to be released from its compressed position," which "impressed the mind of the beholder with the power of omnipotence and the insignificance of human power when compared to that of Nature's God."

By the time Dryer's party climbed the volcano, the crater on the south side, which was described by witnesses to the 1842-44 eruptions, had disappeared beneath snow and the forming glaciers. Dryer did see a crater on the northwest flank and wrote that "smoke was continually issuing from its mouth." In 1854, six months after the ascent, *The Oregonian* updated their coverage, reporting that there was "more smoke issuing from it than there was then, which indicates that the volcanic fires are rapidly increasing within the bowels of this majestic mountain." The last known eruption of this cycle was in April 1857, when the *Washington Republican* reported from Steilacoom that the peak had "for the last few days been emitting huge volumes of dense smoke and fire, presenting a grand and sublime spectacle."

During the late 1850s volcanoes were the least of the problems facing the newcomers to the Northwest wilderness. Isaac Stevens, the governor of the newly-formed Washington Territory, forced treaties and reservations on the Northwest tribes, but gold rushes led to the invasion of the remaining Indian lands by miners and settlers. In 1855-56 open war broke out

between the white settlers and the natives. Led by Chief Kamiakan of the Yakimas, the Klickitats and their allies attacked Seattle and Fort Rains, an Army post in the Columbia Gorge. Then an expedition of 200 Indians crossed the Klickitat Trail, but the "rebels" were sighted by "Indian Zack," who was hunting at Chelatchie Prairie and who warned the settlers living southwest of the volcano; they fled to safety across the Columbia. Even though the tribes west of Mount St. Helens were too decimated to resist the immigrants, most of the homesteads there were hastily deserted. By 1860, when the second known ascent of the volcano was made, the Indian resistance had waned; the settlers returned, and their thoughts turned to gold.

The August 1860 visit to the summit of Mount St. Helens is thoroughly described in an amusing booklet, *Gold Hunting in the Cascade Mountains,* written under the pseudonym of Loo-wit Lat-kla. The book mocks the "periodical attacks of 'gold fever' which has frequently prompted small companies and individuals to start out and spend days and weeks in prospecting the large and small sand bars of Lewis River, and the deep gulches of its tributaries, for the precious deposits which, to their excited imagination, lay hid but a little way beneath the surface." The hordes of prospectors would fail to find the "color" and soon return to their farms and settlements — but would always claim that they were going back to the goldfields "next week."

The book also relates a tale about an earlier attempt to climb Mount St. Helens. Some employees of the Hudson's Bay Company finally found an Indian guide willing to take them up to timberline, but when the party was part way up the Lewis River, a sudden rainstorm drenched them. Half of the men wanted to return home, and the guide refused to proceed further without more blankets. The men who wanted to continue on threatened to shoot the native guide, but he was protected by the mutineers. Finally, the disgruntled explorers gave up and returned to civilization, forfeiting what could have been a first ascent.

The 1860 climb of the volcano was made by a group of six settlers who headed up the Lewis River to hunt elk, prospect for gold and "rusticate awhile." They followed the Simcoe (Klickitat) Trail up the river past the homesteads at the lush "Cha-la-cha-Prairie," but the men soon bored of prospecting in the Lewis River "diggings." Reasoning that the gold hunting would be better farther up the side-streams, the party found a Klickitat Indian, John Staps, who finally agreed to "pilot" them through the thick undergrowth on Mount St. Helens' steep ridges up to the base of the volcano. After a long, torturous climb, the party found the peak "standing like a hoary-headed giant amongst an army of dwarfs." On a bed of lava called "She-quash-quash," the guide and his companion were appalled by the tourists' irreverent noise and predicted that the Great Spirit would, as always, retaliate with a storm. According to the author: "Greatly rebuked were some of us who had been cursing the way, when these untutored savages told us that they had too much reverence for the Spirit, and were too

Discovered in 1895 by settler Ole Peterson, Ole's Cave is a 1½-mile long lava tube which formed on the southwest side of the mountain just north of the Lewis River. Nearby Ape Cave, over 2-miles long, is one of the world's longest lava tube caves. The caves were formed when the outer surfaces of lava flows cooled and hardened, while the fluid lava below the crust drained away. *Photo by the Kiser Brothers, 1903/Courtesy Oregon Historical Society.*

much awed by this evidence of His mighty power, to laugh and talk foolishly in the sight of Him who had devastated the traditional hunting ground of their fathers." To the chagrin of the infidels, "rain soon began to pour down in torrents."

At timberline the Indians left the others and headed "toward a beautiful prairie of some three thousand acres, lying on the top of the ridge to the southwest, where mountain sheep, black-tail deer and woodchuck are numerous." The pioneer party continued on toward the summit, finally reaching it after climbing for hours. The bad weather broke, and the author, unaware of Dryer's climb, declared that "the top of Mount St. Helens ceased to be a *Terra incognita*." The Columbia and Willamette Rivers (in those pre-smog days) "looked like streaks of silver on a groundwork of velvet," and the vista was "the most gorgeous, the most sublimely grand, picturesque and wonderfully attractive spectacle upon which the eye of man ever feasted." The "yawning crater" seen by Dryer was still visible on the north slope, but it had become as "cold as the snow around it."

The author seemed to find religion atop the volcano and "felt as if nothing was easier than to soar from crag to crag and from peak to peak, but the intense cold served to bring us to reason again, and make us feel that we were yet in the *flesh*." During the descent, the party almost slid into a huge crevasse. Unlike the other cracks in the glacier, this chasm "increased in width as far down as we could see, probably 300 feet, assuming the form of an inverted funnel." When steam rose from the crevasse, the author asked if there could still be "some latent fire, an embryo volcano, struggling into life and activity"; he predicted that "we may yet live to witness another eruption of Mount St. Helens."

The exhausted climbers reached the timberline camp after sunset, and the Indian guides cooked two deer and a huge woodchuck. The guides "predicted a tremendous storm, and admonished us to hurry from the mountain before it came upon us, because the Tie [God] was mad and meant to punish us for our invasion of his domain." The party wanted to go to Spirit Lake next — but changed their minds when "the most terrific rain storm I ever witnessed came down upon our pathway, saturating everything." Snow suddenly covered the peak from timberline to the summit. The adventurers headed home, but their travels were made hazardous by floods.

Upon the climbers return home, the other pioneers were primarily interested in whether or not any gold had been found, but the Klickitat Indians "were greatly exercised" by the rumors of an ascent of "Loo-wit-lat-kla." When the tribe heard that one of their own had guided the expedition, they were sure that their people would be "punished, if not destroyed" because of the trespass. "Fearing the storm raised round his ears," John Staps, the guide, denied any participation; he "probably saved his *bacon* by his resolute persistence in asserting a lie; but the Indians still look upon our party with suspicion." The Klickitats were not destroyed, but they were sent to the Yakima Reservation east of their homeland.

Mount St. Helens remained almost "terra incognita" for decades, although a few more people climbed it before the next turn-of-the-century. The crater on the north slope disappeared beneath glaciers sometime between the McBride ascent of 1874 and the 1883 climb by a group which included the first women to reach the summit. The first ascent via the north side was probably made in 1893 by Colonel Plummer's party, whose guide, Leschi, was one of the first Indians to break with tradition and visit the top of the mountain-god.

The Northern Pacific Railroad was completed from Kalama to Tacoma in 1873 and stimulated the development of the region west of Mount St. Helens. Kalama and Centerville (Centralia) boomed in the 1870s, the first store in Woodland opened in 1881, and Kelso was platted in 1884. The town of Toutle was founded in 1876; logging of the watershed followed a decade later, and a logging railroad was built up the valley in 1895. In the Lewis River watershed, Yale was founded in 1867, the Speelyai mill opened in 1890, and the company town of Yacolt was established a short time later.

Many visitors came to Mount St. Helens to hunt elk on the partially-wooded lava fields above the Lewis River. Ole Peterson, a Cougar pioneer, found the first of the lava tube caves on the volcano's south side while hunting deer in 1895. Ole's Cave soon became a popular tourist attraction — as did Ole. (Most of the numerous other local lava caves were not found until after World War II.)

Development — recreational and otherwise — arrived slowly at Mount St. Helens; the peak was remote from navigable waterways, the rugged canyons surrounding it were nearly impassable, and eruptions were still within recent memory. Robert Lange homesteaded downriver from Spirit Lake in 1879 and built a trading post; Marsh and Hofer were also early settlers in the area. Mining began just north of the volcano in 1891, two years after Washington became a state, and the St. Helens Mining District was established in 1892. Pressure from prospectors led County Commissioner Studebaker to build the first wagon road from Castle Rock to Spirit Lake in 1901. Dr. Henry Coe, who had previously worked at an "Alaska sanatorium for the insane," bought out early mining claims and even sold stock to Teddy Roosevelt. Lange traveled to Germany, where he borrowed a quarter million dollars to develop his claims next to Coe's. Barges were used to haul machinery and ore across Spirit Lake. A fire at Lange's mine in 1908, started by the smudge pots miners used to keep flies off their horses, burned the forest on the south side of Mount Margaret. Interest in the mining area fizzled out by 1911, although some gold, silver, copper and other metals have been taken out over the years. Mining claims continued to be filed, primarily to gain ownership of the timber.

Mount St. Helens was first included in a federal forest reserve in 1897 and became part of Columbia National Forest in 1908, during a period of huge forest fires. The U.S. Forest Service built a guard station at Spirit Lake in 1910 and a ranger station in 1913; a fire lookout was later constructed atop the mountain. The Spirit Lake—Trout Lake trail was blazed in the early 1900s, but most of the region's trails were built in the

1930s by the Civilian Conservation Corps (CCC). Four youth camps, beginning with the Portland YMCA camp, were located on the shoreline of Spirit Lake, as were a few private resorts and many private cabins. Public campgrounds were built at the lake in the 1930s. Coe's Dam raised the level of Spirit Lake a couple of feet, and three large power-generating dams were built on the Lewis River just south of the volcano.

With road access to Spirit Lake, and later to Timberline, climbing Mount St. Helens became a popular pastime in the Northwest, especially among outdoor clubs such as the Portland-based Mazamas and the Mountaineers from Seattle. The 1908 Mazamas' climb turned into an ordeal, but it had a heroic ending. The summit wasn't reached until sunset, and the seven-hour descent had to be made in darkness—with all 25 members hanging onto the same rope across the icefields! After the climbers returned to their base camp at Spirit Lake, two Swedish loggers straggled in seeking help for a companion, whose leg had been broken by a falling rock. Charles Forsyth and six other Mazamas returned with the loggers and finally found the injured man near timberline on the south slope. Since there was then no easy exit to the south, the men had to build a stretcher and carry their patient over the moun-

tain during the night and down the north side to the road. Forsyth Glacier was named in recognition of this rescue.

Meanwhile, Mount St. Helens remained *almost* quiet. In 1898 the *Seattle Post-Intelligencer* reported that "great volumes of smoke are emitting from its crater"; the local people felt "great consternation" and were "naturally much excited and somewhat alarmed" at first, but the incident was soon forgotten. Five years later, three people caught in a storm near timberline heard a "terrible explosion," followed by "a violent trembling of the earth" and "a hailstone of rocks and dust." The 1903 eruption was "so severe" that the party was "thrown to their knees, rocks were hurled in different directions and the trees swayed to and fro as if in a hurricane." Another minor eruption took place in the winter of 1921. Newlyweds Mr. and Mrs. Claude Crum told the *Kelsonian* that they were in a cabin at Spirit Lake when "it became as dark as night early in the afternoon and there was a terrific electric storm." Three days later, however, they "were making the rounds of their trap line" and found that the mountain's north and northeast slopes "were dark with a fine powder like cinder dust."

Despite these "supernatural" occurrences and the fumaroles and warm spots near The Boot on the north slope,

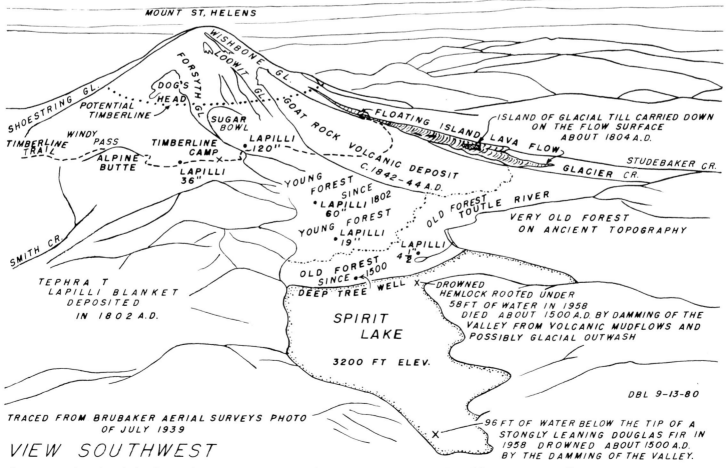

Illustration of north side landscape history prior to 1980 volcanic activity. *Courtesy Donald B. Lawrence Collection.*

By tree ring analysis in 1939, Donald B. Lawrence discovered several years of suppressed growth and established that there had been a major eruption of pumice from Mount St. Helens about 1802. Geologists have now designated this deposit as the Tephra T Layer. *Photo by Donald B. Lawrence.*

1810

1802

1801

1800

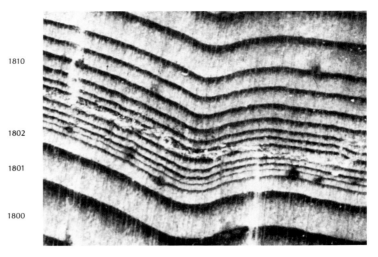

local residents were generally more interested in Sasquatch, alias Bigfoot, than in vulcanism. Indian stories told of huge, ape-like creatures in these woods, but the current Bigfoot legends began in 1924, when a group of hairy giants reputedly attacked six miners on Mount St. Helens. The miners claimed that they shot one of these creatures and it fell into a deep ravine (forever-after known as Ape Canyon). A search party from Kelso and Longview failed to find the Sasquatch's body, but — according to some sources — the miners' cabin had been destroyed by large boulders thrown by the beasts. Huge footprints found around the mountain in the following years caused much excitement — and brought in reporters and tourist dollars — until it was discovered that all of the prints were of the same right foot.

A new road from Castle Rock to the lake was opened in 1939 and was paved in 1946. A paved road to Timberline was finished in 1962 to provide access to a planned downhill ski resort, but avalanches made the project impractical.

The name of the national forest surrounding Mount St. Helens was changed in 1949 to honor the founder of the U.S. Forest Service, Gifford Pinchot, who had died three years earlier. Extensive clear-cutting and road-building in the forest began shortly thereafter. In 1949 there were 655 miles of roads in the national forest; by 1980 there were 3700 miles — and few roadless areas remained for hikers and wildlife (and water storage). The mileage of trails plummeted; over half of them were converted to logging roads. The people who once visited Spirit Lake and St. Helens for the solitude and beauty were increasingly confronted with denuded vistas, motorboats on the lake, and snowmobiles and other off-road vehicles almost everywhere else. Most of the fireworks surrounding the volcano in the three decades previous to the 1980 eruptions were between conservation organizations on one side and logging companies and off-road vehicle owners on the other.

The U.S. Forest Service admits that "timber harvesting has been quite extensive" at St. Helens, but the agency and the timber industry claim that the large cut is needed to provide lumber and jobs and that clear-cutting is an economic necessity. The management of the Gifford Pinchot around the volcano is complicated by the checkerboard of private lands — primarily owned by Weyerhaeuser, Burlington Northern, Peterman Mfg. and Champion International — within the national forest. (Burlington Northern, through 19th century government land grants to railroads, even owns the crater of Mount St. Helens.) These private inholdings are generally even more economically-utilized than the publicly-owned sections, where the U.S. Forest Service at least limits the size of the clear-cuts.

The political pressure on the Forest Service to increase cutting is overbearing since the local counties receive a large share of the revenues from Forest Service timber sales to compensate for the fact that property taxes are not collected on public lands. For example, Skamania County, which encompasses most of Mount St. Helens, annually receives over $1000 per county resident from the Forest Service. Conser-

vationists counter that cutting in the Gifford Pinchot is far above the "sustained-yield" level, which provides a continuous supply of timber, and that the harvestable trees will soon be gone, leaving the counties without their main source of income until the forest grows back. The timber industry answers that it will compensate by greatly-increasing the growth rate of the trees through intensive management, including the widespread use of herbicides to eliminate competing shrubs. Conservationist organizations reply that such schemes are largely impractical and are converting multi-use forests into single-use tree farms.

The clear-cutting has moved swiftly up Mount St. Helens' tributaries, including timber along streams and on lands where the Forest Service admits that the regeneration (regrowth) potential for trees is nil. The expensive efforts to replant the timberline clear-cuts have failed; once the pioneer vegetation has been destroyed, the pumice becomes a desert in summer. Conservationists say that most areas around the mountain, such as the heavily-logged Toutle and Kalama River valleys, were devastated *before* the recent eruptions. Only the north side of the mountain (where the blast damage was most intense) remained in a semi-natural state by 1980, and chainsaws were even closing in on the gem of the area, Spirit Lake. Also, the lands on the mountain's westernmost flanks — owned primarily by logging conglomerates and the State of Washington's Department of Natural Resources — are in even worse shape than the national forest lands (a major reason why there is so much pressure to cut the federal timber). Mount St. Helens was also (and may again be) threatened by renewed mining activities, such as the open-pit copper mine planned on the north side by the Duval Corporation.

When Mount St. Helens erupted, local conservationists were working to protect and restore the area around the mountain within a national monument or scenic area administered by the National Park Service. The new eruptions will only intensify this effort, based on the precedent that the other active volcanoes in the United States became national parks or monuments soon after they erupted. Ironically, shortly before "Loo-wit" dramatically returned to life, a noted conservationist, pleading for the protection of Washington's "gentler, more vulnerable Southern Cascades," wrote that the Northern Cascades were largely protected by their ruggedness, but around Mount St. Helens, "nature must depend heavily upon man with a sensitivity toward wild lands to come to her defense."

Above, top: Charles W. Embody escorted his twin nieces from the East around timberline on Mount St. Helens in 1897 or 1898, for "an experience they would never forget." The nieces and two Chinese coolies (in straw hats) are shown crossing the Floating Island Lava Flow. The coolies were brought to clear a path for the horses. Above: This photo of the party boating on Spirit Lake shows remnants of three drowned trees — the result of a volcanic mudflow about 1500 A.D., which raised the lake's level over 60 feet. *Both photos by Charles W. Embody/Courtesy Donald B. Lawrence Collection.*

Above: The Oregon Alpine Club, the first outdoor club to ascend the mountain, reached the summit on July 26, 1889. This photograph of the party is probably the first picture ever taken on the summit. The earliest recorded ascent was made by Thomas J. Dryer and three others in 1853. *Photo by A. C. Warner/ Courtesy Northwest Collection, University of Washington.* Opposite, top: With alpenstocks for balance, members of the Mountaineers club slide down snow-covered slopes to avoid the loose rocks of the talus ridges. Opposite, bottom: Dwarfed by the mountain, a single-file of 46 Mountaineers executes a switchback while ascending Mount St. Helens on August 8, 1917. Overleaf: After five days in camp, the 52 members of the 1917 annual outing eat breakfast before departing their timberline camp for Mount Adams. *All photos: Courtesy The Mountaineers.*

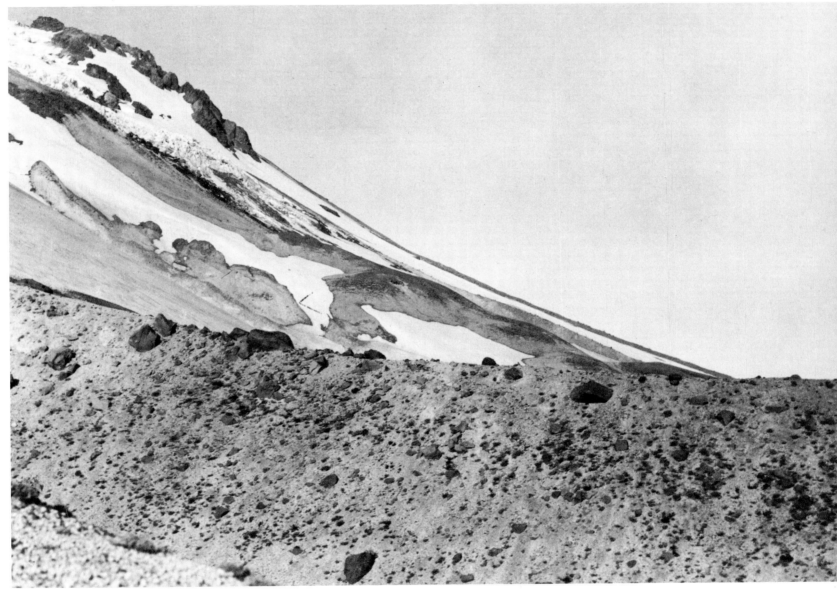

Above, top: Eating lunch on The Boot in 1917, the Mountaineers found the warm rocks "a happy choice in the icy breeze that prevailed." This talus ridge near the top contained active fumaroles — and was all that remained of the north side crater and thermal area last described in 1874. *Photo by H. W. Player.* **Above:** Chimney Rock on the south rim stood sentinel as the party crossed the snow-filled summit crater. The tent sheltered the Forest Service crew which was building the lookout cabin. *Both photos: Courtesy The Mountaineers.*

Above, top: Holmstadt Memorial Lodge was built by the Portland Young Men's Christian Association (YMCA) on the south shore of Spirit Lake in 1928; it could accommodate fifty people. The YMCA, which first began outings to the lake in 1909, relocated its camp to the north shore in 1946. The Episcopal Diocese of Olympia acquired the old camp and used it until the 1970s, when the buildings were removed because of high upkeep costs. *Courtesy Portland YMCA.*
Above: The Mountaineers visit the resident forest ranger in 1917. The U.S. Forest Service built a guard station at Spirit Lake in 1910 and in 1913 established district headquarters at the lake. *Courtesy The Mountaineers.*

Above, top: Robert C. Lange began his homestead in 1879, one mile down the Toutle River from Spirit Lake. A wagon road was built to the lake in 1901, just nine years after the area became a mining district. Lange established a trading post at his homestead, and a telephone line reached it in 1906. Above: In 1925 a Packard full of Mazamas on a Fourth of July outing found the road little improved. *Courtesy U.S. Forest Service.*

Above, top: This view of the south shore is from the outlet of Spirit Lake. When Thomas Dryer climbed the peak in 1853, he wrote that Spirit Lake looked "like a splendid jewel in an enamelled setting, as it reflected the beautiful deep green shadows of the surrounding forest." **Above:** Mazamas pose in 1925 on an ore barge beached near the Sweden Mine. The barge was built in the winter of 1901-1902 to carry machinery and ore across Spirit Lake; remnants were still visible in 1979. *Both photos: Courtesy The Mazamas.*

Above: Climbers rest near the framework of the Forest Service lookout cabin, which was built on the summit of Mount St. Helens during the summer of 1917. *Courtesy The Mountaineers.* Above, top: The cabin featured extra reinforcement against heavy snow and a glass-enclosed cupola with a firefinder. Haze and bad weather conditions caused poor visibility at this elevation, so the lookout was last manned in the summer of 1927; it was boarded up in 1928. *Photo by C. L. Marshall/Courtesy The Marshall Collection.* Opposite, top: A party of Mountaineers (self-described as "seekers of the high places, those of the strong backs and weak minds") are shown approaching the lookout. *Courtesy The Mountaineers.* Opposite, bottom: Climbers were treated to hot coffee and homemade donuts by S. George Schnitgler, the "blue-eyed, red-haired" lookout stationed atop the mountain in 1922. *Courtesy The Mountaineers.* Overleaf: The northwest face of the mountain included the Toutle and Talus glaciers and the canyon of the South Fork of the Toutle River, a vast V-shaped trench cut into the soft pyroclastic and avalanche deposits by the glacial streams. *Photo by Donald B. Lawrence, 1940.*

Top (both pages): These photos, taken at 4500 feet on the Plains of Abraham, on the east side of Mount St. Helens in 1897 by Kellogg (opposite page) and 1940 by Lawrence (above), show how the timberline was advancing toward the climatological limit (about 6500 feet at this latitude), *Courtesy Donald B. Lawrence Collection.* **Opposite, bottom:** The *circa* 1802 eruption deposited an eight-foot layer of frothy pumice (the light grey band directly below the woman) near timberline on the north slope. **Above:** Conifers stand on the 3½-mile-long Floating Island Lava Flow, which was extruded about 1804 from beneath the Wishbone Glacier on the northwest flank. All of the features pictured here were obliterated in May 1980. *Both photos by Donald B. Lawrence.* **Overleaf:** 12,276-foot Mt. Adams rises to the east of Mount St. Helens in this view from Dog's Head. The two peaks were frequently confused by early observers. *Photo by Ray Atkeson.*

Above: Spirit Lake (foreground) was the "emerald gem" of the region, but its origin was from mudflows across its west end. On the north slope of the mountain are vestiges of other volcanic activity, including the dacite dome of Goat Rocks (with its debris fan created during the 1842-1844 eruptions), Sugar Bowl Dome and Dog's Head. **Opposite:** Both logging and recreational activities flourished around the mountain's flanks—often competing with each other and conflicting with conservationists' desires for preservation of this unique area and protection of the watersheds. The cabin was located at Harmony Falls Lodge. **Overleaf:** The cabins at Harmony Falls provided a breathtaking view of both lake and mountain. *All photos by Ray Atkeson.*

Preceding pages: Climbers on the Toutle Glacier enjoyed an inspiring view of the countless valleys of the Cascade Range. *Photo by Ray Atkeson.* Opposite: A climber dressed in the alpine gear of the 1940s perches on a *serac* (huge blocks of glacial ice) overlooking the Toutle River. *Photo by Ray Atkeson.* Above, top: In this 1954 photo, Boy Scouts and other vacationers wait on the south shore dock for a boat ride to the north end of Spirit Lake. The boat arriving was the *Tressa,* a former Russian lifeboat put into service by Harmony Falls Lodge in 1946; it was still in use in 1980. *Photo by Walt Dyke.* Above: Portland YMCA members enjoyed many campfires at Camp Meehan on the north shore. *Photo by Ray Atkeson.*

Opposite: Swimmers plunge into the chilly waters of Spirit Lake at the Portland YMCA camp. Buildings of the original camp are visible across the lake on the south shore. *Photo by Ray Atkeson.* **Above, top:** The vapor temperature of this fumarole on the west side of The Boot was measured at 190° F. on July 13, 1941. The Boot bordered on the Forsyth Glacier, the area of the bulge just prior to the May 18, 1980 eruption. *Photo by Donald B. Lawrence.* **Above:** From the northeast side, the Dog's Head is directly below the false summit, while Goat Rocks is on the far right horizon. *Photo by Donald B. Lawrence.* **Overleaf:** Winter snows glisten on the north face at Timberline Viewpoint. Avalanches made a planned downhill ski area impractical on these slopes. *Photo by John Gronert.*

Opposite: The symmetrical cone of Mount St. Helens as seen from Oregon across the Columbia River. Lt. Kautz observed in 1858 that St. Helens, Mount Adams and Mount Hood rose above the clouds, "looking like pyramidal icebergs above the ocean." *Photo by James Mason.* **Above, top:** Campers enjoyed the Mount Margaret backcountry north of Spirit Lake. This backpackers' paradise included centuries-old trees, small lakes, alpine meadows and rock-crested ridges. *Photo by John Marshall.* **Above:** This view of the north face of Mount St. Helens at sunset was taken from Mount Rainier. *Photo by Art Wolfe.* **Overleaf:** Rising behind the Tatoosh Range, Mount St. Helens and its glaciers were visible from Paradise in Mount Rainier National Park. *Photo by Ed Cooper.*

Opposite: The roar from Harmony Falls attracted hikers and boaters alike as it echoed across Spirit Lake. *Photo by Walt Dyke.* Above, top: The Portland YMCA's Camp Meehan will continue to live in the memories of the thousands who had the opportunity to enjoy its facilities and outdoor programs over the years. The Portland Boy Scout and Girl Scout camps and the Southwest Washington YMCA camp also provided unforgettable experiences. *Photo by Duane Rhodes.* Above: Island Lake's pristine water and wooded shoreline was typical of the Mount Margaret backcountry lakes, where fishermen cast for rainbow, cutthroat and eastern brook trout. *Photo by John Marshall.* Overleaf: On the Lewis River south of the mountain, Yale Lake (shown here), Swift Reservoir and Lake Merwin provide recreation as well as hydroelectric power. The headwaters of the Lewis and Cowlitz Rivers are east of Mount St. Helens, since they existed before the mountain formed. *Photo by Ray Atkeson.*

Opposite: Salmon and steelhead migrated from the Pacific Ocean up the Toutle River to Spirit Lake. Summer steelhead were successfully introduced into the Toutle in the 1960s. *Photo by Ray Atkeson.* Above, top: The ramp at Duck Bay provided boaters access to Spirit Lake, elevation 3199 feet. The two-mile-long lake was two and one-half miles wide and as much as 184-feet deep. *Photo by Dallas Swogger.* Above: Boot Lake formed between the steep rocky ridges of the backcountry. Mount Rainier looms on the horizon. *Photo by Ray Atkeson.*

Above: The forest around Mount St. Helens was once an unbroken expanse of evergreens, including Douglas fir, Noble fir, Pacific silver fir and western red cedar. *Photo by Art Wolfe.* Above, top: A hiker leans against one of the rare 400-year-old Douglas firs in the Green River valley, a dozen miles north of the mountain. The seven-mile stretch of virgin trees was one of the largest stands of old-growth Douglas firs still left in the Cascades, and a bitter controversy was raging over its future. Four miles of this remnant forest, shielded by a ridge, survived the May 18 eruption. *Photo by Russ Jolley.* Opposite: A small stream flows past a western red cedar in the Green River backcountry. *Photo by John Marshall.*

Above: A cross-country skier ventures onto frozen Spirit Lake. *Photo by Walt Dyke.* **Opposite:** Climbers work their way up the Forsyth Glacier and then rest in the summit crater under Chimney Rock. On weekends with favorable weather, it was not uncommon for 500 people to make the relatively easy ascent by various routes. *Both photos by Russell Lamb.* **Overleaf:** Climbers are dwarfed by seracs on the Forsyth Glacier, one of the two largest glaciers on the mountain. (Shoestring Glacier had extended down to the 4800 foot level, the lowest glacial tip on the mountain.) Mount Adams is on the horizon. *Photo by Don Lowe.*

Above: Most of the visible cone of Mount St. Helens, seen here across Spirit Lake, had formed within the last few hundred years. **Opposite:** The youthful symmetry of Mount St. Helens was obvious when compared to the sculpted and eroded 75,000-year-old cone of Mount Rainier. Both peaks are composite volcanoes *(stratovolcanoes)*, composed of alternating layers of lava flows and fragmental deposits (ash, breccias, etc.). *Photos by Don Lowe.*

Pages 72-73: On March 27, 1980, after a week of earthquakes around the mountain (sometimes more than 100 per day greater than magnitude three), ash-laden steam broke through the cracking ice crown and opened a new 250-foot wide crater. Opposite: That eruption rose 7000 feet into the air, and shortly thereafter government officials closed the plowed road to Spirit Lake and Timberline Viewpoint. *Both photos by Al Hayward.*

BORN AGAIN

The cycle of eruptions that began in 1980 was not really unexpected. Noting its "long history of spasmodic explosive activity," government geologists familiar with Mount St. Helens had written that it was "probably the volcano most likely to endanger people and property in the western United States." They and other geologists had predicted an eruption before the end of the century — but had found little public or governmental interest in the warning. The Cascade Range is a chain of volcanoes, many of them only dormant; eruptions are inevitable. In fact, the current period of relative calm may be abnormal.

The perimeter of the Pacific Ocean is dotted with volcanoes, the *Ring of Fire*. Scientists now think that the earth's surface is composed of huge *tectonic* plates floating on *plastic mantle,* and the plate below the Pacific is expanding, forcing itself beneath the surrounding continental plates. The crust being forced down into the earth's hot mantle melts, turning into magma which works itself up through fissures in the plates, to form mountains such as the Cascade Range. When pressure builds up from heated gases (mostly steam) below the surface, it is released through powerful volcanic eruptions.

Mount St. Helens is a young volcano, an adolescent. Although it formed atop an older volcano, dating back over 36,000 years, the visible cone is thought to have formed a few thousand years ago, long after nearby rivers were flowing and people were living in the region. The upper cone is only a few hundred years old and is still changing. Even the peaceful lakes around the mountain were born of volcanic violence. Spirit Lake formed when mudflows blocked the headwaters of the Toutle River, and the lake level was raised over 60 feet by mudflows about 1500 A.D. Merrill Lake southwest of the volcano was also created in the same manner.

Mount St. Helens' pre-eruption uniqueness was a result, primarily, of its youth. (It is also west of the Cascade Range, making it first in line for storms that pour in off the Pacific Ocean.) The older volcanic cones along the Cascades were buried beneath glaciers during recent Ice Ages, and the rivers of ice gouged and reshaped the peaks' soft silhouettes. Since St. Helens' cone was built long after the most recent Ice Age, glaciers and erosion have only begun to sculpture it.

Unlike the other Cascade volcanoes, which are famed for their wildflower displays, Mount St. Helens had virtually no alpine meadows even before this eruption. And timberline on the mountain is only about 4000 feet above sea-level, far below what is normal at this latitude. Few plants can colonize the recent pumice since it doesn't retain moisture. Merrill Lake and some of the mountain's glaciers don't even have outlet streams; the water seeps into the pumice, ash and fractures in the lava, and then emerges elsewhere as springs.

The 1980 eruption cycle had a rather innocuous beginning on March 20th, when scientists recorded a strong earthquake around Mount St. Helens. During the next week, the earthquakes increased rapidly, arriving in swarms and causing avalanches. Then, on March 27th a loud boom announced the first eruption; a cloud of steam and ash rose 7000 feet into the sky, and a small crater — about 250 feet wide — opened atop the awakening mountain. A second opening soon appeared, and the two craters kept enlarging until they merged into one large hole about 1700 feet across and 850 feet deep.

There were occasional steam and ash eruptions during April and early May — to the delight of the many sightseers. The earthquakes moved upward from ten miles deep in the earth to about sea-level, and scientists noticed harmonic tremors, vibrations thought to be magma moving deep in the volcano. By early May the area around The Boot, where climbers had once warmed themselves, was bulging out at a rate of five feet per day. As the north side swelled, The Boot moved up and north more than 320 feet, and steam and ash eruptions were increasingly common. The top of the volcano was coming apart, and huge cracks appeared. The south side of the summit remained stable, but the north side pulled away, moving mainly outward. Mount St. Helens was literally bursting at the seams.

Then, on the morning of May 18, after a couple of quiet days, earthquakes triggered a massive landslide; much of the north face slid down the mountain. With the confining weight — the lid on the volcano — gone, the slide released a tremendous lateral blast that decimated everything in its path. Next the summit exploded, sending an ash plume over 60,000 feet into the air, blocking the sunlight. Lightning bolts shot out of the billowing cloud.

The blast and pyroclastic flows (avalanches of hot gases and rock debris) leveled all trees for 17 miles to the northeast, and the heat scorched many more at its edge. Mudflows, fueled by the melting snow and ice, caused extensive flooding, especially along the Toutle River; the temperature of the Toutle rose to about 100° F. Spirit Lake was again enlarged and turned into a mudhole. The blast blew all of the water out of some lakes and killed the mountain's goats and ptarmigans, millions of fish and birds, thousands of deer and elk, and dozens of people. The insect die-off was extensive, causing starvation among fish and birds, even in eastern Washington. The ashcloud drifted around the world, and falling ash stopped normal activities for hundreds of miles to the northeast.

The eruptions diminished over the next few days, but a week later, on May 27th, another major eruption filled the sky. Then, on June 12th, when the winds had changed, ash from yet another major eruption fell on Portland, Oregon, and western Washington. A lava dome formed in the crater, but was blown away — a cycle that will surely be repeated. More eruptions — large and small — followed sporadically.

U.S. Geological Survey scientists, who have studied the volcano for decades, wrote in 1978 that "future eruptions of Mount St. Helens are near certainty" and "it will not be possible to prevent, or to stop them after they have begun." Their statements are still true.

Above: A small steam eruption obscures the features of Mount St. Helens on April 4; harmonic tremors, probably indicating the movement of magma below the volcano began April 1 and continued infrequently. Such tremors may be helpful to scientists in predicting future eruptions. *Photo by John Marshall.* **Opposite:** The dark ash from the first eruptions absorbed sunlight in mid-April, causing avalanches and ice flows around the Sugar Bowl and elsewhere on the mountain. *Photo by Ralph Perry.*

Above: The prevailing winds from the Pacific Ocean blow steam emissions eastward on March 28; that evening, "blue flames" were first observed in the crater. *Photo by John Marshall.* **Opposite:** The March 30 eruption threw huge blocks of ice (visible in picture) into the air. Earthquakes, measuring up to 4.9 on the Richter Scale, continued to crack the summit; there were 79 earthquakes on March 30 alone. *Photo by Dave Olson.*

Above: A steam eruption, increasingly filled with dark ash, breaks through a lenticular cloud in early April. *Photo by Al Hayward.* Opposite, top: By early May, the initial crater and a second one had merged and enlarged into a single large crater (over 1700 feet across and 850 feet deep), and the north face (foreground) had bulged out more than 320 feet. *Photo by Al Hayward.* Opposite, bottom: The crater occasionally vented steam, but was relatively calm from April 23 to May 6. *Photo by Glen Finch.*

Opposite: By April the weather had cleared enough for volcano-watching to become a favorite pastime in the Pacific Northwest. *Photo by Chuck Williams.* **Above:** Snow and blocks of ice crumbled from the stable south wall of the crater as the restless north side swelled and pulled away from it. *Photo by Al Hayward.* **Overleaf:** The moon rises over Mount Adams as another small eruption continues to cover the east side of Mount St. Helens with ash. *Photo ©Dr. James L. Lee/Earth Images.*

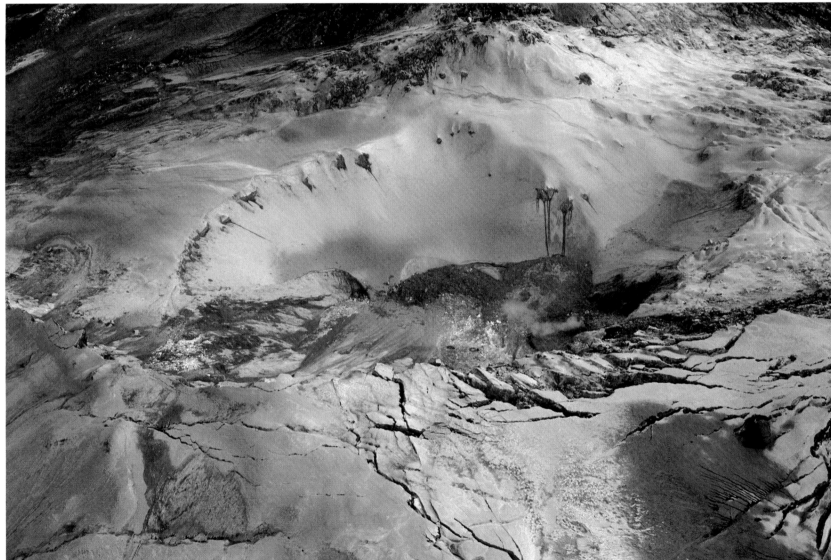

Opposite: At approximately eight o'clock (PDT) on the morning of May 18, 1980, avalanches and ice flows were observed on the swollen, fractured north face from a plane 1300 feet above the summit. **Above:** This photograph, taken about 8:10 a.m., clearly shows water seeping from the north wall and a small lake forming in the crater. **Above, top:** At 8:32 a.m. an earthquake of 4.9 Richter magnitude started ice avalanches on the south wall of the crater and rippled the north slope (lower right corner), triggering a massive landslide. **Overleaf:** The landslide rumbled down toward the Toutle River valley from the crater (upper left corner) as an ashcloud exploded out a thousand feet down the north face. *All photos ©K & D Stoffel.*

These four photographs, taken seconds apart, were shot from Bear Meadows, 12 miles northeast of the mountain, and recorded the beginning of the explosion which blew over half a cubic mile of Mount St. Helens into the air. The initial landslide was still moving down the mountain when a vertical eruption, dark with ash, burst from the summit and a larger lateral blast blew out what remained of the north face. The lateral blast overtook the landslide and buried everything within four miles to the north. Super-heated ash clouds and shock waves caused further devastation up to seventeen miles from the volcano. *All photos ©Gary Rosenquist/Earth Images.* **Overleaf:** *The vertical eruption blew steam and ash 60,000 feet into the air and continued throughout the day. Photo by Glen Finch.*

Below: Viewed from the 11,000 foot level on Mt. Rainier's Nisqually Glacier, 55 miles to the north, the high velocity of the lateral blast is evident compared to the slowly rising ash cloud. *All photos by Richard Anderson.* Opposite: Eight minutes after the eruption, a wall of ash overtakes a tree-lined ridge thirteen miles northeast of the mountain. *Photo by Keith Ronnholm.*

Opposite: Viewed from the west, the morning sun was quickly blocked out by the oncoming ash cloud. *Photo by Bea Johnston.* **Above, top:** The ash cloud fans out down the Toutle River valley, as shown in this view from the Spirit Lake highway (Hwy 504). *Photo by Bea Johnston.* **Above:** By early evening much of the mountain top had disappeared; the crater continued to enlarge throughout the night. *Photo by Gary Braasch.*

Opposite: This classic photo, taken at 10:00 a.m. on May 18, 1980, shows the tremendous ash cloud during the early stage of the eruption. *Photo by Roger Werth/Woodfin-Camp.* **Above:** Numerous pyroclastic flows during the day reached temperatures over 500°F (250°C) and speeds up to 200 mph. *Photo by James Mason.* **Overleaf:** The Toutle River mudflow, a product of melting glaciers and snow, left a long trail of thick, hot mud down the valley (as viewed the following day). The resulting floods silted the lower Cowlitz and Columbia Rivers. *Photo by Glen Finch.*

Opposite: The main cloud is momentarily cloaked in steam around its base during the early stages of the eruption on May 18. **Below:** Along the southwest lip of the crater, a curl of ash approximately fifty feet high is sucked back into the main column, unable to descend the slope due to the enormous updrafts. *Both photos by Bruce Curtis.*

Opposite: The ash curl is shown in a closer view. *Photo by Bruce Curtis.* **Above, top:** A steaming mudflow, clocked at 50 mph, surges down the Toutle River valley, engulfing everything in its path. It was one of several mudflows that day. *Photo by Roger Werth.* **Above:** Late in the day a second plume rose (left) from the vicinity of Spirit Lake. *Photo by Russell Lamb.*

Mount Hood

elevation 3,199 feet
Spirit Lake
elevation 3,400 feet

elevation 9,677 feet
Mount St. Helens
elevation 8,400 feet

Mount Adams

Above: In this April 17, 1980 view of the ash-covered south side, Mount St. Helens stands 9,677 feet high. **Opposite:** The May 18 eruption reduced the mountain to 8,400 feet. *Both photos by Ron Cronin.*

Inside Foldout: These before-and-after panoramas were taken from the same place on a ridge 1800 feet above the east arm of Spirit Lake in April and August 1980; both images were made at 7:30 a.m. *Both photos by Michael Lawton/Cirama.*

Mount Margaret backcountry

The changing landscape is shown in these before-and-after pictures taken from an altitude of 60,000 feet. With infrared (heat-sensitive) film, living vegetation appears red, and dead vegetation appears purple. The rectangular patches in both photos are clear cuts from extensive logging. The blast area and mudflows are visible in the "after" picture; steam covers the crater. Both photos by NASA-Ames Research Center/Courtesy U.S. Forest Service.

Goat Mountain

"NATURAL" DISASTERS

California has its earthquakes, the Midwest its tornadoes; Atlantic and Gulf Coast shoreline cities have their hurricanes, and now the Northwest has to contend with its volcanoes. The volcanoes have been present all along, of course, but their decades-long hibernation, a short nap in geologic time, had lulled the burgeoning Northwest population into complacency. No more—at least for a short time. The recent history of people soon forgetting the forces behind "natural" disasters is not encouraging.

Volcanoes may be disastrous, but life would not exist without them. Volcanoes have erupted for billions of years, and they belched forth the atmosphere and water that made life possible on this planet. Volcanic activity gave the Northwest most of its beauty and mineral richness, and the fertile farmlands in eastern Washington are the result of vulcanism. Volcanoes are so powerful and unpredictable, however, that they should be treated with respect, maybe even—taking a lesson from the natives of the area—with religious awe.

Landscapes that are repeatedly altered by volcanic eruptions, floods, hurricanes, earthquakes and other sudden shows of nature's powers are best used for outdoor recreation, agriculture and scientific study; developing them extensively is gambling with big stakes. In recent decades scientists have learned much about determining which areas are high risk, but political sensibilities have rarely kept up with scientific knowledge. The 1980 eruption of Mount St. Helens is a dramatic reminder that geology is not limited to the ancient past.

A park of some kind will be established around Mount St. Helens; the question is how large the park will be and which agency will manage it. On the other hand, there will be salvage logging of downed trees; again the debate is over how much and where. The U.S. Forest Service has already declared the immediate area around the volcano a "geological area," but conservation organizations, pointing to what they consider the Forest Service's previous mismanagement of the area, will no doubt push for a national park or monument managed by the National Park Service. (Previous to the recent eruptions, the Forest Service had protected less than two thousand acres around the mountain as "Natural Research Areas.") Immediately after the May 18 blast, the Forest Service announced plans to begin salvage logging, and the Soil Conservation Service began seeding with non-native grasses — without consulting with the general public.

The other volcanoes that erupted this century—Katmai in Alaska, California's Lassen Peak and the shield volcanoes in Hawaii—are now managed by the National Park Service. Although their management in some areas is often similar, the missions of the U.S. Forest Service and the National Park Service are very different. National forests are open to extractive uses—such as logging, mining, grazing and hunting—but are supposed to be managed to provide for the greatest long-term benefits for the general public, the citizens who own the forests. The purpose of national parks and monuments, which encompass a much smaller part of the country than do national forests, is preservation—the protection of natural areas, historic sites and native plants and animals.

The distinction between the agencies has become somewhat blurred in recent years as newer types of units—such as national recreation areas, scenic areas and preserves — are established. Buildings and internal-combustion engines are banished from Forest Service wilderness areas, but grazing, hunting and mining are allowed. Hunting, grazing, farming and even oil and gas extraction are permitted in some new units of the National Park System, such as national preserves and recreation areas. These "compromise" parklands, including complexes combining wilderness and lightly-developed lands, will be increasingly-important models as the country's wild lands and natural resources continue to shrink.

When President Carter visited the volcano after the May 18 eruption, he predicted that Mount St. Helens will rival Grand Canyon National Park as a tourist attraction. The most important reasons for establishing parks and wilderness areas, however, are to protect natural diversity (they are invaluable "genetic banks") and aid scientific study of natural processes. As scientists watch the future actions of Mount St. Helens and the "recovery" of the surrounding landscape, they will learn much about the history of the Cascades — and will have a better understanding of what the future holds for residents of the restless Northwest and other people living near volcanoes.

It will be easier to determine what kind of protective area should be established around Mount St. Helens than it will be to settle on what should be done about threatened communities downstream from the volcano. The town of Castle Rock, for example, is built atop a mudflow. Lava has flowed into the Lewis River canyon within the past 2000 years, and mudflows raised the level of Swift Reservoir two feet in 1980. Government geologists predict that "if a volcanic event led directly or indirectly to the failure or overtopping of Swift Dam, a catastrophe could result."

The stickiest problem, of course, is what to do about existing developments within the hazard areas; but the fate of future developments must also be decided. Recent history is not encouraging. Developers are still building subdivisions on earthquake faults, floodplains and other dangerous areas. For example, cities built upon barrier islands are repeatedly devastated by hurricanes; but the causes of these "natural" disasters are usually forgotten within a generation.

Meanwhile, the molten heart of the volcano will still continue to throb — no matter what human beings do to its surface. Mount St. Helens is still a young mountain, and — despite the major setback in 1980 — it will probably grow again, possibly higher than the other snowy cones that tower above the ever-changing Cascade Range. And it will continue to change the surrounding landscape.

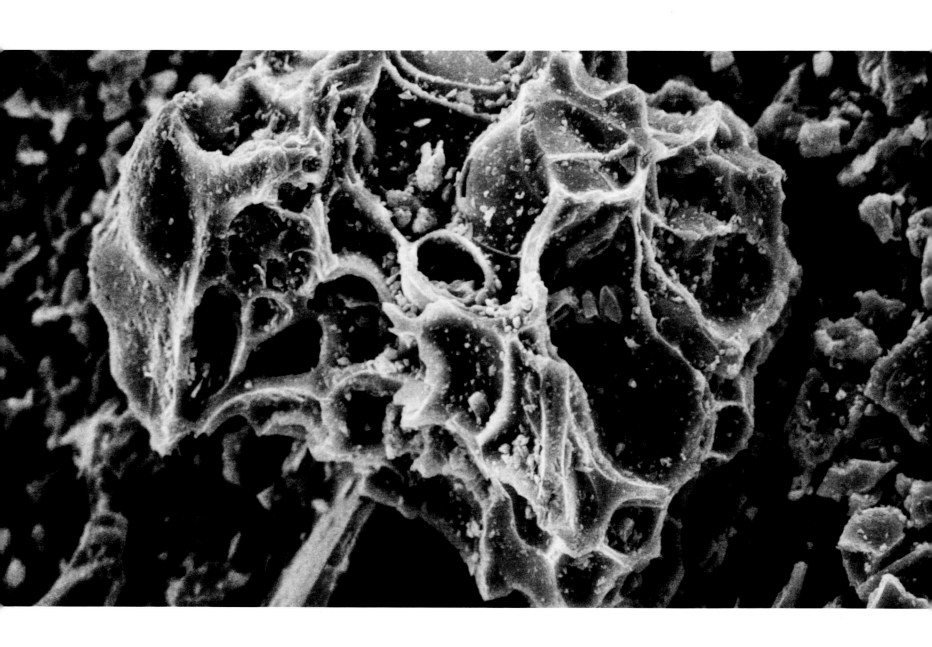

Opposite: Magnified 2500 times by an electron microscope, a speck of pumice ejected from Mount St. Helens reveals the tiny cavities caused by gas *(vesicles)* which give the volcanic rock its buoyancy. *Photo by W.H. Fahrenbach.* **Above, top:** Mudflows raised the level of June Lake, located on the southeast flank of the mountain, and flooded young Douglas fir trees. *Photo by Ron Cronin.* **Above:** As water came into contact with superheated pyroclastic debris, steam blasts created phreatic explosion craters around the old outlet of Spirit Lake. This large one, now cooled and inactive, is approximately 200 feet across. *Photo by Gary Braasch.*

Opposite: A damaged fir tree clings to a slope above Spirit Lake. Decaying vegetation will provide nutrients for new growth. *Photo by Gary Braasch.* **Above, top:** A hoof print left by a wandering Roosevelt elk testifies to survival in the ash, but thousands of elk died, decimating one of the largest herds in Washington. *Photo by Ron Cronin.* **Above:** Beargrass seedlings push their way through the ash, returning life to the land. Fireweed has also begun to colonize the barren landscape, and will be followed by the windblown seeds of other "weeds" and grasses. Insects and small rodents will move in after the plants, and soil will again form. *Photo by Ron Cronin.* **Overleaf:** The symmetrical upper cone of Mount St. Helens was replaced by a huge amphitheater nearly two miles long, one mile wide and about 4000 feet deep. A lava dome has plugged the vent. *Photo by Jim Mason.*

Opposite: Cracked by pressure beneath it, the lava dome reveals its hot, molten interior. *Photo by Ancil Nance.* **Above:** An ash cloud from a mid-summer eruption drifts eastward; carried by the winds, it will reach parts of Canada and the eastern United States. *Photo by Gary Braasch.* **Overleaf:** The now-barren summit of Mount St. Helens will again be covered with snow and carved by ice. Before the 1980 eruptions of Mount St. Helens, 90% of the government funds for the study of volcanic hazards went for the Hawaiian volcanoes. *Photo by Gary Braasch.*

Above: As the initial ash cloud reaches high winds and spreads, a second eruption billows upward from the volcano. *Photo by Jay McAlonen.* **Opposite:** A full moon rises over the new crater. The forces of nature are clearly in evidence, and change remains the only constant. *Photo by Gary and Becky Vestal.*

SELECTED BIBLIOGRAPHY

Atkeson, Ray. *The Cascade Range.* Portland: Graphic Arts Center, 1969.

Becky, Fred. *Cascade Alpine Guide, Climbing and High Routes, Columbia River to Stevens Pass.* Seattle: The Mountaineers, 1973.

Bennett, Edith Page. "The Mount Adams, Mount St. Helens and the Goat Rocks Outing." *The Mountaineer* Vol. 15, No. 1 (Dec. 1922).

Bigelow, Alida. "Mount Saint Helens, the Youngest of the Volcanoes of the Cascades." *The Mountaineer,* Vol. 10, No. 1 (Dec. 1917).

Bunnell, Clarence. *Legends of the Klickitats.* Portland: Binford & Mort, 1933.

Buzzetti, Beatrice. "The Mount St. Helens Area." *Cowlitz County Historical Quarterly,* Vol. 4, No. 4 and 5 (1963).

Clark, Ella. *Indian Legends of the Pacific Northwest.* Berkeley: University of California Press, 1953.

The Columbian staff. *Mount St. Helens Holocaust.* Lubbock: C. F. Boone, 1980.

Crandell, Dwight and Mullineaux, Donal. *Potential Hazards from Future Eruptions of Mount St. Helens Volcano* (Bulletin 1383-C). Washington, D.C.: U.S. Geological Survey, 1978.

The Daily News and *Journal-American* staffs. *Volcano.* Longview: Longview Publishing Co./Madrona Publishers, 1980.

Farmer, Harris and Carson. *Mt. St. Helens Volcanic Weatherbook.* Portland: Mountain Graphics, 1980.

Harper, Russell. *Paul Kane's Frontier.* Austin: Univ. of Texas, 1971.

Harris, Stephen. *Fire and Ice.* Seattle: The Mountaineer/Pacific Search Press, 1980.

Hazard, Joseph. "The Guardians of the Columbia." *The Mountaineer* Vol. 25, No. 1 (Dec. 1932).

Holmes, Kenneth. *"Mount St. Helens' Recent Eruptions." Oregon Historical Quarterly* Vol. 61, No. 3 (Sept. 1955).

Jerman, Jerry, and Mason, Roger. *A Cultural Resource Overview of the Gifford Pinchot National Forest, South-Central Washington.* Seattle: Univ. of Washington, 1976.

Kiser Bros. *Pacific Coast Pictures.* Portland: Wonderland Souvenir Co., 1904.

Korosec, Rigby and Stoffel. *May 18, 1980 Eruption of Mount St. Helens.* Olympia, Washington State Dept. of Natural Resources, 1980.

Lawrence, Donald. "Continuing Research on the Flora of Mt. St. Helens." *Mazama* Vol. 21, No. 12 (1939).

Lawrence, Donald. "Diagrammatic History of the Northeast Slope of Mt. St. Helens, Washington." *Mazama* Vol. 36, No. 13 (1954).

Lawrence, Donald. "The 'Floating Island' Lava Flow of Mt. St. Helens." *Mazama* Vol. 23, No. 12 (1941).

Lawrence, Donald. "Trees on the March." *Mazama* Vol. 20, No. 12 (1938).

Loo-wit Lat-kla (pseudonym). *Gold Hunting in the Cascade Mountains.* Vancouver (W. T.): L. E. V. Coon, 1861.

Majors, Harry. "Mount St. Helens Series." *Northwest Discovery* Vol. 1, No. 1 (June 1980) and No. 2 (July 1980).

McConnell, Grant. "The Cascade Range" and "Mountaineering." *The Cascades* (Roderick Peattie, ed.) New York: Vanguard Press, 1949.

The Oregonian staff. *Mount St. Helens, The Volcano.* Portland: Oregonian Publishing Co., 1980.

Phillips, Kenneth. "Fumaroles of Mount St. Helens and Mount Adams." *Mazama* Vol. 23, No. 12, (1941).

Ray, Verne. "Handbook of Cowlitz Indians." *"Coast Salish and Western Washington Indians III.* New York: Garland Publishing, 1974.

Sterling, E. M. *The South Cascades: The Gifford Pinchot National Forest.* Seattle: The Mountaineers, 1975.

U.S. Forest Service. *Green/Spirit Planning Unit.* Vancouver: Dept. of Agriculture, 1978.

Verhoogen, Jean. *Mount St. Helens, a Recent Cascade Volcano.* Berkeley: Univ. of California, 1937.

Warre, Henry. *Sketches in North America and the Oregon Territory.* Barre, Mass.: Imprint Society, 1970.

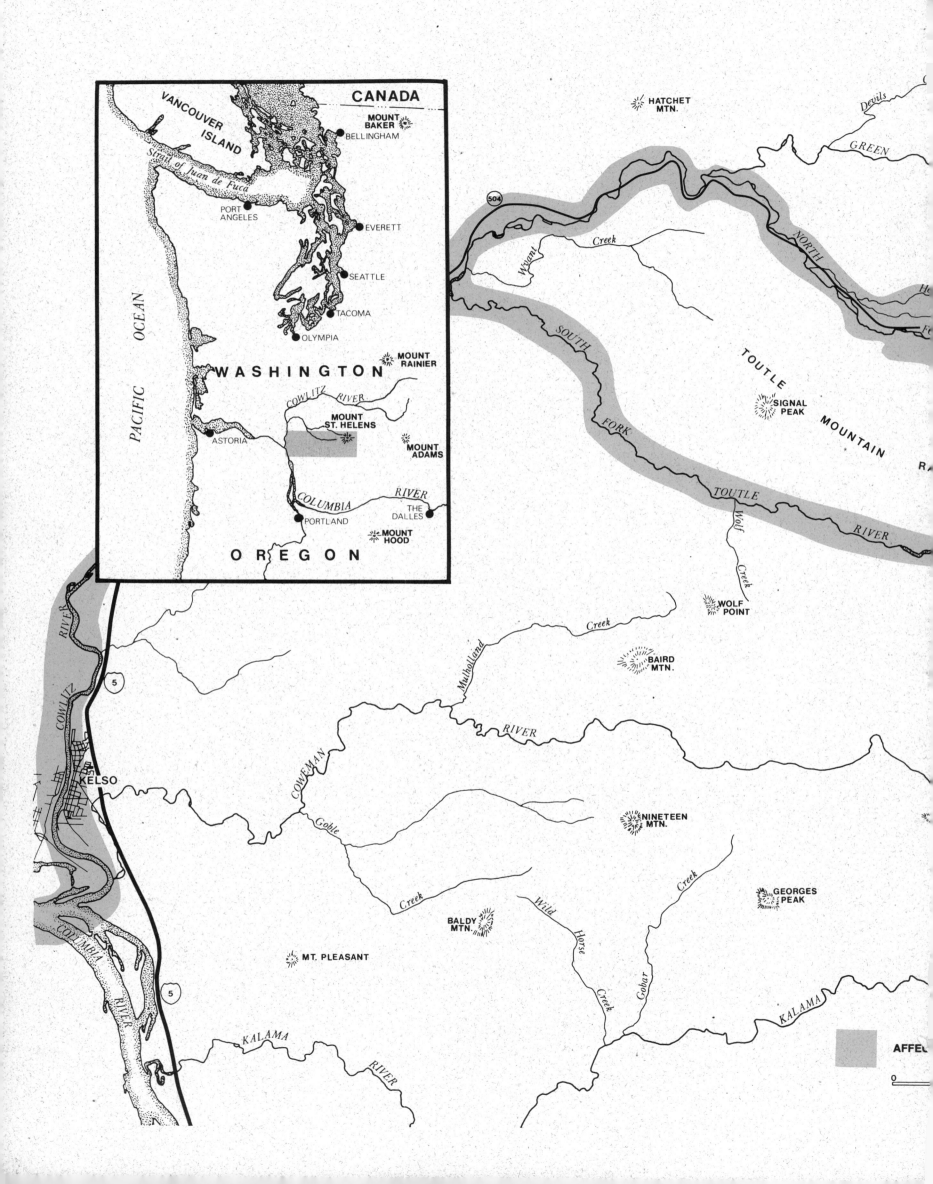

CANADA

VANCOUVER ISLAND

Strait of Juan de Fuca

MOUNT BAKER
BELLINGHAM

PORT ANGELES

PACIFIC OCEAN

EVERETT

SEATTLE

TACOMA

OLYMPIA

WASHINGTON

MOUNT RAINIER

COWLITZ RIVER

MOUNT ST. HELENS

ASTORIA

MOUNT ADAMS

COLUMBIA   RIVER

THE DALLES

PORTLAND

MOUNT HOOD

OREGON

HATCHET MTN.

Devils

GREEN

504

Wyant   *Creek*

NORTH

He

SOUTH

TOUTLE MOUNTAIN

SIGNAL PEAK

FORK

TOUTLE

Wolf

RIVER

RA

Creek

WOLF POINT

RIVER

Creek

Mulholland

BAIRD MTN.

RIVER

Coweman

NINETEEN MTN.

Goble

Creek

GEORGES PEAK

Creek

Wild

BALDY MTN.

Horse

Creek

Gobar

MT. PLEASANT

KALAMA

AFFEC

KALAMA

RIVER

KELSO

5

COWLITZ

RIVER

COLUMBIA

RIVER

5

0